MR. POTATO HEAD INVENTOR

INVENTOR

George Lerner

PAIGE V. POLINSKY

Checkerboard Library

An Imprint of Abdo Publishing
abdopublishing.com

abdopublishing.com

Printed in the United States of America, North Mankato, Minnesota
062017
092017

THIS BOOK CONTAINS
RECYCLED MATERIALS

Design and Production: Mighty Media, Inc.
Editor: Liz Salzmann
Cover Photographs: Courtesy of the Ellman family (center); Mighty Media, Inc. (border)
Interior Photographs: Alamy/Disney Pixar/Entertainment Pictures, p. 25; Courtesy of the Ellman family, p. 13;
Courtesy of The Strong®, Rochester, New York, pp. 5, 8, 9, 14, 15, 17, 19, 21, 24, 28 (both), 29 (bottom);
Darth Ray, p. 27 (top left, bottom left & bottom right); iStockphoto, pp. 12, 27 (top right & bottom center), 29 (top);
Shutterstock, pp. 11, 22, 23, 29 (center)

Publisher's Cataloging-in-Publication Data
Names: Polinsky, Paige V., author.
Title: Mr. Potato Head inventor: George Lerner / by Paige V. Polinsky.
Other titles: George Lerner
Description: Minneapolis, MN : Abdo Publishing, 2018. | Series: Toy trailblazers |
    Includes bibliographical references and index.
Identifiers: LCCN 2016962800 | ISBN 9781532110962 (lib. bdg.) |
    ISBN 9781680788815 (ebook)
Subjects: LCSH: Lerner, George, 1922-1955--Juvenile literature. | Mr. Potato Head
    (Toy)--Juvenile literature. | Toymakers--United States--History--Juvenile
    literature. | Inventors--United States--Biography--Juvenile literature.
Classification: DDC 688.7/092 [B]--dc23
LC record available at http://lccn.loc.gov/2016962800

CONTENTS

Chapter 1
YOUNG *Spud*

For hundreds of years, a war has raged on. All over the world, parents face off against their children. The battlefield is the dinner table. The war cry? "Don't play with your food!" But in the 1950s, a new toy appeared in stores. Not only did it encourage kids to play with their food, but it gave them special tools to do it. And what was more, parents didn't mind!

Mr. Potato Head gave kids a whole new way to play. Today, the toy includes a plastic head that kids can add features to. But the original Mr. Potato Head just included the features. Kids added them to real potatoes!

This toy sensation was invented by George Lerner. He was born in 1910 and grew up in Brooklyn, New York. George had two younger sisters. But little else is known about George's childhood or family. Some say that George's toy **legacy** began when he was a young boy.

According to the story, George took vegetables from his mother's garden. He stuck

FUN FACT

Today, many people collect Potato Head items. A man in Birmingham, Alabama, has nearly 1,000 of them!

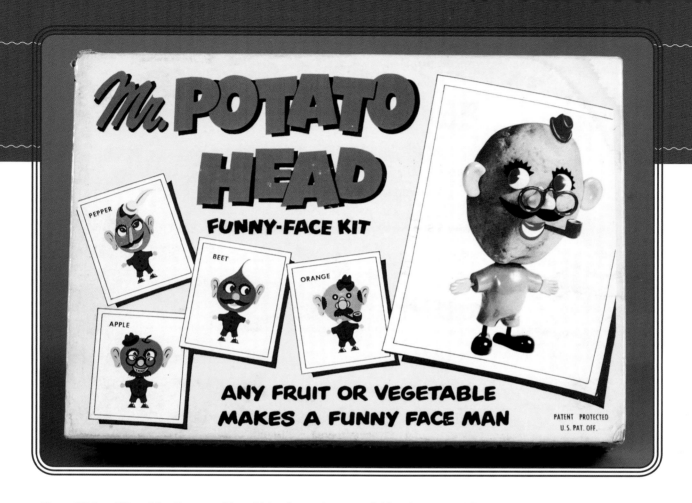

Over 100 million Mr. Potato Head kits have been sold in the past 60 years!

small items into them to turn them into dolls. George then gave these dolls to his sisters. Whether this story is true or not, one thing is certain. George would grow up to become a toy trailblazer!

Chapter 2

Food FUN

George became an artistic, creative adult. In the 1930s, Lerner worked as a toy designer for a toy company in Illinois. It was called the Buddy L Manufacturing Company.

Buddy L made toys out of pressed steel. In 1939, the company faced a major challenge. That year, **World War II** began. The US government needed a lot of metal to produce weapons, **ammunition**, and other goods for the military. So, Buddy L and many other US companies had to stop using metal for their products. Part of Lerner's job at Buddy L was to change the toy designs from metal to wood.

By 1949, Lerner had started a family. He and his wife, Faye, had two sons, Franklin and David. At dinnertime, Lerner's sons often played with their food. Telling them to stop didn't work. So Lerner came up with a new plan.

Lerner gathered bottle caps, thumbtacks, and other items. He stuck them into potatoes, giving the potatoes silly faces. Franklin and David

FUN FACT

In 1986, Mr. Potato Head received four write-in votes during the Boise, Idaho, mayoral election.

loved the potato faces. They now had food other than their dinner that they could play with! Playing with the potato dolls was a lot less messy. Lerner decided to further develop his idea. He believed other children would enjoy the potato faces as much as his sons did.

Lerner created many toys during his lifetime. Mr. Potato Head was by far the most famous.

TO JUNE & JULIE
WITH VERY BEST
WISHES—LOVE—

Chapter 3

Potato PROTOTYPE

Lerner quickly got to work on the potato faces toy. He created plastic face pieces including eyes, ears, and noses. They had plastic spikes that could be pushed into potatoes. Lerner completed his **prototype** in 1951 and called it the Funny Faces for Food kit.

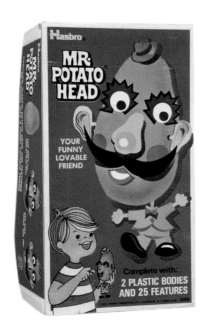

Lerner's kit was not the first toy for creating silly faces. Other toys with movable facial features existed and were popular. But Lerner was **confident** his Funny Faces kit would stand out. His was the first kit to include **3-D** pieces. It was also the first to use food! Lerner knew his idea was **unique**. He just needed to find a toy company willing to **market** it.

Finding a buyer was harder than Lerner expected. He presented the kit to several companies. But nobody was interested. They

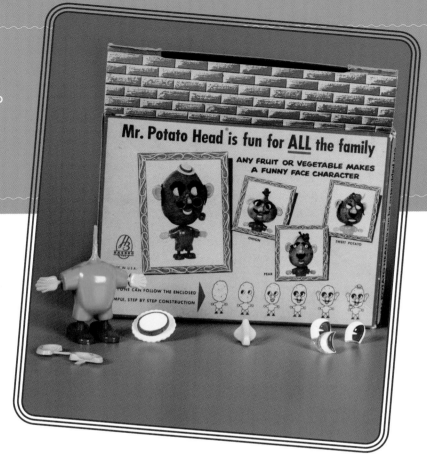

were mainly concerned about the toy's use of vegetables. It seemed like a waste of food.

Food had been scarce during **World War II**, which had ended just a few years earlier. Parents would remember having to get by with less food. How could any company sell them a toy that wasted food? Many thought the Funny Faces kit would be impossible to **market**. Even Lerner's old workplace, Buddy L, turned him down. But Lerner didn't give up.

Chapter 4

CEREAL *Star*

After two years of searching, Lerner finally found a buyer. In 1951, he sold Funny Faces to food company Post Cereals. The company paid Lerner $5,000 for the idea. But Post wasn't going to sell the kits on their own. Instead, Funny Faces would be used to advertise breakfast cereal.

Funny Faces pieces were included in cereal boxes as special prizes. It wasn't what Lerner had hoped. But it was the best deal he could find. Little did Lerner know, a better opportunity would come along soon.

A few months after Lerner's Funny Faces were released, they caught the attention of Henry Hassenfeld and his son Merrill. Henry and Merrill owned the Hassenfeld Brothers company. Henry had started the company in 1923 with his brothers, Hillel and Herman. The company name was later shortened to Hasbro.

Hasbro was a toy company. It sold play kits of themed **accessories**. Depending on the kit, kids could pretend to be doctors, mail carriers, makeup artists, and more. Hasbro's play kits

FUN FACT

Mr. Potato Head has his own Facebook page.

While not as common today, prizes in cereal boxes were a big deal in the 1950s. At that time, most cereal boxes contained prizes!

were successful. Now Henry and Merrill were looking for new toys to add to the company's collection. They loved the Funny Faces cereal prizes and believed the idea could be turned into a popular toy.

Henry and Merrill met with Lerner. They told him they loved his Funny Faces kits. Unlike the other toy company executives, the Hassenfelds weren't worried about wasting food. Unfortunately, the Hassenfelds were too late. Lerner's idea already belonged to Post Cereals. But the Hassenfelds were determined. They made a deal with Post.

Hasbro is the third-largest toy maker in the world! It is known for Mr. Potato Head, G.I. Joe, My Little Pony, and more.

George Lerner and the Lernell Company developed many toys throughout the years. The company is now run by Ellman (*pictured*) and his sons.

Post Cereals returned the rights to Lerner for the $5,000 they paid him, plus $2,000 from Hasbro. In 1952, Lerner sold his Funny Faces kits to Hasbro.

While Lerner was developing his Funny Faces kit in 1951, he started a toy company with his friend Julius Ellman. The two men combined their names and called the business Lernell Company. Lerner and Ellman enjoyed a successful partnership for more than 30 years. Meanwhile, Hasbro was developing Lerner's Funny Faces kit idea.

Chapter 6

Hot POTATO

Hasbro changed the name of the Funny Faces kit to Mr. Potato Head. The company released the toy in 1952. Mr. Potato Head came with 30 plastic pieces. This included four noses and two pairs of eyes. Kids could also choose from three hats, eight hair pieces, and more.

The Hassenfelds wanted to create excitement for their new toy. And they knew just how to do it. Televisions were becoming very popular. Many companies had started **marketing** their products using TV ads. But every commercial was aimed at products adults used. After all, adults were the ones who had the money to buy products!

Hasbro decided to try something different. The company produced the first commercial in TV history to advertise a toy. Not only that, but the ad spoke directly to child viewers.

Early Mr. Potato Head kits included a booklet with funny face ideas kids could try.

It **described** Mr. Potato Head as "the most wonderful friend a boy or girl could have." Children saw the toy in action right on the screen. And they wanted it!

At only $0.98 each, the Mr. Potato Head kits were a bargain. And parents had no problem with wasting a potato or two to make their children happy. Within a few months, Mr. Potato Head made more than $4 million in sales. The toy was a hit!

Chapter 7

MR. and Mrs.

Mr. Potato Head's popularity continued to grow over the next year. Children loved creating their own potato pals. They could use their imaginations to make funny new faces. Or, they could change their potato's face to match their own mood. The possibilities were endless!

Hasbro continued to build on Mr. Potato Head's success. It began adding an order form to each kit. These forms advertised 50 additional Mr. Potato Head **accessories**. With help from their parents, children could use the forms to order these extra parts.

Kids loved Mr. Potato Head. But he was all alone. The Hassenfelds knew that a matching toy would be just as popular. So, in 1953, Hasbro released Mrs. Potato Head. The Mrs. Potato Head kit was very similar to the Mr. Potato Head kit. But Mrs. Potato Head came with a purse, earrings, and other stylish accessories. Mr. Potato Head's wife was a huge hit. It was just the encouragement Hasbro needed.

FUN FACT

Mr. and Mrs. Potato Head's official wedding **anniversary** is February 14, Valentine's Day!

Mrs. Potato Head could be purchased on her own or with Mr. Potato Head.

Chapter 8

The Gang's ALL HERE

The Potato Head family quickly grew. Mr. and Mrs. Potato Head soon had two children! Their son was named Spud. Their daughter was Yam. The Potato Heads also got a car, a trailer, and a boat. They even got pets! The "Spud-ettes" kit came with animal face pieces and a helpful booklet. Kids could assemble four different pets by the book. Or they could create their own strange, silly creatures!

Magazine ads displayed the happy family having fun together. It was clear that Mr. Potato Head was more fun with company! In the 1960s, Hasbro introduced a group of friends for the Potato Heads. The Tooty Frooty Friends kit included more than 60 plastic pieces. With them, kids could create characters including Katie the Carrot, Pete the Pepper, and Oscar the Orange.

FUN FACT

In 1968, Hasbro released a Mr. Potato Head on the Moon kit. It included materials to make a Potato Head astronaut, a spaceship, and even aliens!

Mr. and Mrs. Potato Head were the faces of Hasbro. They were even used to market other Hasbro products!

Mr. Potato Head had more pals than ever before! But Hasbro needed something fresh and new to keep kids interested. The company began releasing themed sets. These sets let kids play with the Potato Heads and their friends in all sorts of fun places. They could work on a farm, explore the Wild West, enjoy the circus, and more. By combining kids' imaginations and Hasbro's creative sets, Mr. Potato Head could do anything!

Chapter 9

Spud SAFETY

Trouble appeared in 1964 when parents began complaining to Hasbro. They were finding old, moldy vegetables around their houses. There was another concern, too. The plastic spikes were sharp and could hurt children. Many were starting to worry that Mr. Potato Head was unsafe.

Luckily, Hasbro found a way to solve both problems. The company began including a plastic head and body in each Potato Head kit. Real vegetables were no longer needed. And the heads and bodies had holes in them. The plastic pieces could snap into the holes. So, the pieces didn't need sharp spikes.

Mr. Potato Head's makeover came at the right time. On November 6, 1969, President Richard Nixon passed the Child Protection and Toy Safety Act. The US government could now test toys and ban those that seemed **dangerous**. By 1974, more than 1,500 toys were banned.

Hasbro was determined to keep its Mr. Potato Head products off the list of banned toys. That year, the company combined the head and body into one large lump. Arms were no longer included in new Potato Head kits. The kits had fewer pieces and the pieces were much larger.

The first plastic Mr. Potato Head was smaller and more oval-shaped than today's version. Mr. Potato Head's parts are now five times larger than Lerner's original!

This made children less likely to choke on the pieces. Hasbro was able to continue selling the toys.

Chapter 10

HEALTHY *Habits*

The Mr. Potato Head toys were still popular in the 1980s. At this time, people were focusing more on health issues. Hasbro wanted to make sure its best-selling toy fit with these new attitudes.

One of the health issues that people were concerned about was smoking. Doctors were warning people that it was unhealthy. For years, Mr. Potato Head had come with a tobacco pipe **accessory**. So, in 1987, the toy officially kicked the habit in a public ceremony. An actor in a Mr. Potato Head costume gave his pipe to the US Surgeon General. From then on, the toy kits did not include pipes.

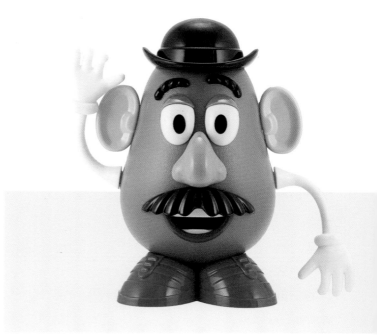

Mr. Potato Head continued to promote good health. In 2005, 2006, and 2007, he wore sneakers and carried a water bottle in the Macy's Thanksgiving Day Parade.

People were also learning more about the importance of exercise. Hasbro **participated** in a promotion to encourage children to be more active. The company announced that Mr. Potato Head was going to exercise. He would no longer be a couch potato! Mr. Potato Head was given an award from the President's Council on Physical Fitness and Sports. Famous actor and bodybuilder Arnold Schwarzenegger presented the award.

Chapter 11

MR. Movie Star

By the 1990s, Mr. Potato Head had become a classic toy. His continued popularity caught the attention of a man named John Lasseter. Lasseter was an **animator** and movie director. In 1991, he started working on an animated film called *Toy Story*. The movie followed the adventures of a group of living toys.

Lasseter wanted to include toys that were classics. This would make the movie more appealing to adults. They would recognize and like the characters right away. One of the toys Lasseter wanted to use was Mr. Potato Head. Hasbro agreed to let Mr. Potato Head be in the movie.

FUN FACT

Mr. Potato Head is the first character seen at the beginning of *Toy Story*.

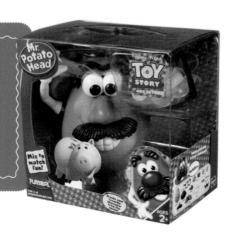

Toy Story was released on November 22, 1995. It was an instant success! After less than two weeks, it earned more than $64 million in ticket sales. And as more people saw the film, toy sales exploded.

Mrs. Potato Head joined her husband in *Toy Story 2*, *Toy Story 3*, and *Toy Story 4*.

After seeing Mr. Potato Head come to life on screen, kids wanted one of their own! Hasbro could hardly keep up with the demand.

Along with the classic kits, the company began releasing Mr. Potato Head key chains, mugs, underwear, and more. Unfortunately, George Lerner never got to see his creation on the big screen. He passed away that very year, before *Toy Story*'s release.

Chapter 12

A Colorful FUTURE

Toy Story showed that children were interested in toys based on movies. So, in 2007, Hasbro produced a movie featuring its Transformers action figures. One of the main characters was a Transformer named Optimus Prime. The company released a Transformers-themed Mr. Potato Head at the same time. It was called Optimash Prime. Kids loved it!

Hasbro began licensing characters from other companies. This allowed Hasbro to add more movie characters to Mr. Potato Head's world. Today, there are more than 30 licensed Mr. Potato Head characters.

At more than 60 years old, Mr. Potato Head continues to inspire children around the world. In 2000, Mr. Potato Head was **inducted** into the Toy Hall of Fame. And George Lerner's contribution has not been forgotten. In 2010, Lerner received a Toy & Game **Innovation** Award from Chicago's Museum of Science and Industry. Thanks to Lerner's creativity, the world is a sillier place.

Potato Head Stars

MR. SPOCK

Star Trek movies
and TV series

DARTH VADER

Star Wars movies

BUGS BUNNY

Looney Tunes
cartoons

SPIDER-MAN

Marvel comics and
Spider-Man movies

IRON MAN

Marvel comics and
Iron Man movies

TIMELINE

1910

George Lerner is born.

1951

Lerner creates the Lernell Company with Julius Ellman. Lerner makes the Funny Faces for Food kit.

1953

Hasbro releases Mrs. Potato Head.

1952

Lerner sells his Funny Faces kit to Hasbro. Hasbro renames it Mr. Potato Head. Mr. Potato Head stars in the first toy commercial on television.

1964

Hasbro starts including a plastic head and body in each Mr. Potato Head kit.

1974

Hasbro combines the head and body into one piece and makes the accessories larger.

2007

Hasbro releases Optimash Prime, the first Mr. Potato Head based on a movie character.

1995

George Lerner dies. Mr. Potato Head stars in *Toy Story*.

2000

Mr. Potato Head is inducted into the Toy Hall of Fame.

2010

Lerner receives a Toy & Game Innovation Award from Chicago's Museum of Science and Industry.

Glossary

accessory – an optional part that adds to the beauty, convenience, or effectiveness of something.

ammunition – bullets, shells, cartridges, or other items used in firearms.

animate – to make using a process that involves a projected series of drawings. They appear to move due to slight changes in each drawing. An animator is a person who creates work using this process.

anniversary – the annual return of the date of a special event.

confident – sure of oneself.

dangerous – able or likely to cause harm or injury.

describe – to tell about something with words or pictures.

induct – to admit as a member.

innovation – a new idea, method, or device.

legacy – something important or meaningful handed down from previous generations or from the past.

WEBSITES

To learn more about Toy Trailblazers, visit **abdobooklinks.com**. These links are routinely monitored and updated to provide the most current information available.

market – to find opportunities to make buyers aware of and want to buy a service or product.

participate – to take part or share in something.

prototype – an original model on which something is patterned.

three-dimensional (3-D) – having three dimensions, such as length, width, and height. Something that is three-dimensional appears to have depth.

unique (yoo-NEEK) – being the only one of its kind.

World War II – from 1939 to 1945, fought in Europe, Asia, and Africa. Great Britain, France, the United States, the Soviet Union, and their allies were on one side. Germany, Italy, Japan, and their allies were on the other side.

Index